JAN 2003

W9-AUO-611

Sitting Bull

By Susan Evento

Consultant
Nanci R. Vargus, Ed.D.
Assistant Professor of Literacy
University of Indianapolis, Indianapolis, Indiana

Children's Press®
A Division of Scholastic Inc.
New York   Toronto   London   Auckland   Sydney
Mexico City   New Delhi   Hong Kong
Danbury, Connecticut

Designer: Herman Adler Design
Photo Researcher: Caroline Anderson
The photo on the cover shows Sitting Bull.

Library of Congress Cataloging-in-Publication Data

Evento, Susan.
  Sitting Bull / by Susan Evento ; consultant, Nanci R. Vargus.
    p. cm. — (Rookie biographies)
  Includes bibliographical references and index.
  ISBN 0-516-21719-4 (lib. bdg.)   0-516-25829-X (pbk.)
  1. Sitting Bull, 1834?-1890. 2. Dakota Indians—Kings and rulers—Biography.
3. Hunkpapa Indians—Kings and rulers—Biography. 4. Little Bighorn, Battle of
the, Mont., 1876. I. Vargus, Nanci Reginelli. II. Title. III. Rookie biography.
  E99.D1 S6036
  978.004'9752—dc22

                        2004000430

©2004 by Scholastic Inc.
All rights reserved. Published simultaneously in Canada.
Printed in the United States of America.

CHILDREN'S PRESS, and ROOKIE BIOGRAPHIES®, and associated
logos are trademarks and or registered trademarks of Scholastic Library
Publishing. SCHOLASTIC and associated logos are trademarks and or
registered trademarks of Scholastic Inc.
1 2 3 4 5 6 7 8 9 10 R 13 12 11 10 09 08 07 06 05 04

Long ago, a Native American chief and his wife had a son. His name was Sitting Bull.

Buffalo

Sitting Bull learned to ride
horses and hunt buffalo.
He hunted buffalo for food.

His people used buffalo skins
to make tepees and clothes.

At age 10, Sitting Bull killed his first buffalo. At age 14, he fought his first battle.

As a man, Sitting Bull fought many more battles.

7

Men looking for gold

In 1868, the United States made a promise to Sitting Bull's people. The United States said that Americans would not take away their land.

Then someone found gold on Indian land. Many Americans came to get gold.

The United States sent people to talk to Sitting Bull's people. They wanted to buy Indian land.

Sitting Bull did not think this was a good idea. His people needed the land to live.

Buffalo once roamed Indian land.

12

Indian leaders knew Americans would not stop coming. So they asked for a lot of money for their land.

The United States said no. Sitting Bull's people were forced to leave their land.

Sitting Bull would not leave.
He and other Indian chiefs made
plans to fight for their land.

15

Sitting Bull's people were ready when the U.S. Army came in 1876.

There was a big battle. It was called the Battle of Little Bighorn. The U.S. Army lost.

The United States took more
Indian land. They also sent
soldiers to make Sitting Bull's
people move.

They were sent to a small area
of land called a reservation
(rez-er-VAY-shun). Sitting Bull
did not go. He took some of
his people to Canada instead.

Indian reservation

20

Too many people had hunted the buffalo in the United States and Canada. Sitting Bull and his people could not find enough to eat.

In 1881, Sitting Bull gave himself up. He and his people came back to the United States.

Sitting Bull was put in jail for two years. After that, he went back to his people on the reservation.

Later, he left to travel with Buffalo Bill's Wild West show. After four months, he went back to the reservation.

A poster for Buffalo Bill's Wild West show

MARY IRVIN WRIGHT

24

A man named Kicking Bear came to see Sitting Bull. He told Sitting Bull his people should do Ghost Dancing.

He said it would help the people be free.

Some Americans were afraid of Ghost Dancing. They thought it would make Sitting Bull's people fight to be free.

The U.S. Army came to take Sitting Bull away. A fight started. Sitting Bull was killed.

Sitting Bull's grave

28

Many people think Sitting Bull was a brave man. He fought to save his people's land. He fought to help his people be free.

Words You Know

Battle of Little Bighorn

buffalo

Ghost Dance

miners

tepee

reservation

Index

About the Author

Susan Evento is a former teacher. For the past 16 years she has been a writer and editor of books and instructional materials. Recently, she was the Editorial Director of *Creative Classroom* magazine, an award-winning K–8 national teacher's magazine. Evento lives in New York city with her partner and three cats.

Photo Credits

Photographs © 2004: Archive Photos/Getty Images: 7; Corbis Images: 4, 30 bottom (Richard A. Cooke), 11 (Ron Sanford), 3, 28; Denver Public Library, Western History Collection: 19, 31 bottom right (B-747), 20 (X-31937), 15 (X-33783); Hulton|Archive/Getty Images: 23; Library of Congress: 16, 30 top (via SODA), cover, 8, 31 top right; National Anthropological Archives, Smithsonian Institution, Washington, DC: 12 (01601906), 5, 31 bottom left (3701); State Historical Society of North Dakota: 27 (0309-027), 24, 31 top left (B0661).